Bond

STRETCH
English
Tests and Papers

9–10 years

Sarah Lindsay

Nelson Thornes

Published in 2013 by:
Nelson Thornes Ltd
Delta Place
27 Bath Road
CHELTENHAM
GL53 7TH
United Kingdom

13 14 15 16 17 / 10 9 8 7 6 5 4 3 2 1

A catalogue record for this book is available from the British Library

ISBN 978 1 4085 1870 0

Page make-up by emc design ltd

Printed in China by 1010 Printing International Ltd

Acknowledgements
The author and the publisher would like to thank the following for permission to reproduce material:

p11 from the Highway Code © Crown Copyright 2012; p20 'The Man from Snowy River' from *Complete Poems* by A.B. (Banjo) Paterson, published by HarperCollins Publisher Ltd Australia (2001); pp21–22 *Martin's Mice* by Dick King-Smith, published by Fox Buster Ltd, an imprint of Penguin Books Ltd (1988). Reproduced by permission of A.P. Watt Literary, Film and Television Agency; pp29–30 adapted from *A Victorian Factory* by Lyn Gash and Sheila Watson, published by Hodder Wayland (1995). Reproduced by permission of Hachette Children's Book; p36 James Reeves, 'The Sea', in *The Collected Poems for Children*, (Heinemann); p36 'Sea Fever' by John Masefield. Reproduced by permission of the Society of Authors; pp42–43 *Wild Swans Three Daughters of China* by Jung Chang © Globalflair Ltd 1991. Published by HarperPress an imprint of HarperCollinsPublishers (1991).

Every effort has been made to trace the copyright holders but if any have been inadvertently overlooked the publisher will be pleased to make the necessary arrangements at the first opportunity.

Introduction

What is Bond?

The Bond *Stretch* series is a new addition to the Bond range of assessment papers, the number one series for the 11+, selective exams and general practice. Bond *Stretch* is carefully designed to challenge above and beyond the level provided in the regular Bond assessment range.

How does this book work?

The book contains two distinct sets of papers, along with full answers and a Progress Chart.

- Focus tests, accompanied by advice and directions, are focused on particular (and age-appropriate) English question types encountered in the 11+ and other exams, but devised at a higher level than the standard *Assessment Papers*. Each Focus test is designed to help raise a child's skills in the question type as well as offer plenty of practice for the necessary techniques.

- Mixed papers are full-length tests containing a full range of English question types. These are designed to provide rigorous practice, perhaps against the clock, for children working at a level higher than that required to pass at the 11+ and other English tests.

Full answers are provided for both types of test in the middle of the book.

How much time should the tests take?

The tests are for practice and to reinforce learning, and you may wish to test exam techniques and working to a set time limit. Using the Mixed papers, we would recommend that your child spends 55 minutes answering the 100 questions in each paper, plus 5 minutes for reading the comprehension extract.

You can reduce the suggested time by 5 minutes to practise working at speed.

Using the Progress Chart

The Progress Chart can be used to track Focus test and Mixed paper results over time to monitor how well your child is doing and identify any repeated problems in tackling the different question types.

Spelling

Write the **plural form** of these words.

1 scarf _____

2 reef _____

3 photo _____

4 crocus _____

5 diagnosis _____

6 muff _____

⬤ 6

> A silent letter can be at the beginning, middle or end of the word.

Write the silent letter found in each of these words.

7 psychic _____

8 kitchen _____

9 surgeon _____

10 thumbscrew _____

11 condemn _____

12 budget _____

⬤ 6

Complete these word sums.

> Watch out! You may need to add a letter.

13 bump + ed = _____

14 ship + ing = _____

15 trek + ed = _____

16 knot + ed = _____

17 croak + ing = _____

18 whip + ed = _____

⬤ 6

Circle the words with a soft c.

> Listen carefully to the sound the c makes.

19–24 necessary   contagious   science

confidence   decision   tolerance

cheetah   exercise   connector

⬤ 6

Rewrite these words correctly.

25 elegent _____

26 haras _____

27 fulfiled _____

28 comparisun _____

29 vicous _____

30 parliment _____

⬤ 6

Now go to the Progress Chart to record your score!   Total ⬤ 30

Focus test 2 Sentences

Write the **tense** that each of these sentences is written in.

Past or present?

1 Let's go to the park on our bikes. _____

2 I did my homework as soon as I got home. _____

3 I went to Legoland and loved it! _____

4 The wind is gusting through the trees. _____

5 I forgot my packed lunch, and was hungry all afternoon. _____

6 The dishwasher needs clearing. _____ 6

Rewrite these sentences, including the missing commas.

You can use commas to highlight a slight pause in a sentence.

7–8 The children ate the cake the biscuits the crisps but not the sandwiches!

_____

9 The Johnson family travelled to Auckland New Zealand and then returned to Australia.

_____

10–11 Jess loved the books *Coraline The Secret Garden The Growing Summer* and *The Silver Sword*.

_____

12 Where have I put my blue goggles that let the water in my stripy swimsuit and beach towel that has a mark on it?

_____

_____ 6

Rewrite each of the following, adding all the missing capital letters.

> Watch out! Not all words will need a capital letter.

13 w j hardiman (name)   _____

14 hong kong (country)   _____

15 *a small pinch of weather* (book title)   _____

16 mrs zucherman (name)   _____

17 *american indian myths and legends* (book title)   _____

18 *harry potter and the philosopher's stone* (book, film and DVD)   _____   6

Rewrite this sentence correctly.

> Make sure that you add all missing punctuation.

19–23 It is freezing outside complained Jake I need my gloves

_____

_____   5

Rewrite these words, adding the missing apostrophes.

24 oclock   _____

25 couldve   _____

26 theyll   _____

27 dont   _____

28 theres   _____

29 were   _____

30 shant   _____   7

Focus test 3 Grammar

Write a more powerful **verb** for each of these verbs.

1 take   _____

2 cut   _____

3 open   _____

4 eat   _____

5 clean   _____

6 break   _____

> Make your verbs as interesting as possible.

6

Sort the **nouns** into the table.

> Watch out, you can only write each noun once!

7–14 Kuwait   axe   hate   pen pal

love   colony   Doughton   host

Proper nouns	Abstract nouns	Common nouns	Collective nouns

8

Underline the **preposition(s)** in each of these sentences.

> A clue to what a preposition is can be found in the word itself.

15–16 Andy climbed over the gate into the field of cows.

17 The hat was blown off his head as the wind gusted.

18 The cat jumped onto the wall to survey her territory.

19 Frankie was sitting in the study doing her homework.

20–21 Beyond the fields, the sun could be seen glinting through the clouds.

7

Write a sentence that includes each of the listed parts of speech.

Underline the part of speech in your sentence.

22 adverb

_____

23 adjective

_____

24 pronoun

_____

25 verb

_____

26 connective

_____ 5

Underline the **adjectival phrase** in each sentence.

An adjectival phrase is a phrase that describes a noun.

27 The freezing, cold, bleak weather encouraged the children to stay indoors.

28 The healthy, red-faced, old gentleman danced through the night.

29 The fast-paced, exciting game lasted for hours.

30 The wet, slimy, stinking mud clung to their boots. 4

Vocabulary

Write the feminine equivalent of each of the following words.

  1 cockerel   _____

  2 duke   _____

  3 grandfather   _____

  4 stallion   _____

  5 buck   _____

  6 groom   _____   **6**

Write an **antonym** for each of these words.

  7 always   _____

  8 answer   _____

  9 artificial   _____

  10 ascend   _____

  11 accurate   _____

  12 admit   _____   **6**

> *Don't get confused with synonyms!*

Write a **definition** for each of these words.

  13 fatigue   _____

  14 vague   _____

  15 dialogue   _____

  16 synagogue   _____

  17 monologue   _____

  18 prologue   _____   **6**

Write the short form often used for each of these words.

19 mathematics   _____

20 newspaper   _____

The shortened form of a word is usually very familiar.

21 telephone   _____

22 advertisement   _____

23 introduction   _____

24 internet   _____

6

Complete each of these expressions with the words below.

An expression is a phrase used in everyday language.

the other foot.   shirt on.

a bug in a rug.   come to an end.

into the wound.   the wrong tree.

25 All good things   _____

26 Barking up   _____

27 The boot is on   _____

28 Rub salt   _____

29 Keep your   _____

30 As snug as   _____

6

This is an extract from the 'Highway Code'. The Highway Code sets out rules for <u>all</u> road users. These points detail information for cyclists.

Rules for cyclists

59 *Clothing. You should wear*
- a cycle helmet which conforms to current regulations, is the correct size and securely fastened
- appropriate clothes for cycling. Avoid clothes which may get tangled in the chain, or in a wheel or may obscure your lights   5
- light-coloured or fluorescent clothing which helps other road users to see you in daylight and poor light
- reflective clothing and/or accessories (belt, arm or ankle bands) in the dark

60 At night your cycle **MUST** have white front and red rear lights lit. It **MUST** also be fitted with a red rear reflector (and amber pedal reflectors, if manufactured   10 after 1/10/85). White front reflectors and spoke reflectors will also help you to be seen. Flashing lights are permitted but it is recommended that cyclists who are riding in areas without street lighting use a steady front lamp.

64 You **MUST NOT** cycle on a pavement.

66 You should   15
- keep both hands on the handlebars except when signalling or changing gear
- keep both feet on the pedals
- never ride more than two abreast, and ride in single file on narrow or busy roads and when riding round bends   20
- not ride close behind another vehicle
- not carry anything which will affect your balance or may get tangled up with your wheels or chain
- be considerate of other road users, particularly blind and partially sighted pedestrians. Let them know you are there when necessary, for example,   25 by ringing your bell if you have one. It is recommended that a bell be fitted

67 You should
- look all around before moving away from the kerb, turning or manoeuvring, to make sure it is safe to do so. Give a clear signal to show other road users what you intend to do (see 'Signals to other road users')   30
- look well ahead for obstructions in the road, such as drains, pot-holes and parked vehicles so that you do not have to swerve suddenly to avoid them. Leave plenty of room when passing parked vehicles and watch out for doors being opened or pedestrians stepping into your path
- be aware of traffic coming up behind you   35
- take extra care near road humps, narrowings and other traffic calming features
- take care when overtaking (see Rules 162–169)

68 You **MUST NOT**
- carry a passenger unless your cycle has been built or adapted to carry one   40
- hold onto a moving vehicle or trailer

Answer these questions.

  1 When riding a bike, what should you wear once it gets dark?

_____

2–3 What type of clothes do you need to wear when cycling in general?

_____

_____

  4 On which date were pedal reflectors made obligatory on new bikes?

_____

5–6 When riding a bike, who should you be considerate to? State the rule number and appropriate quote from the extract.

_____

  7 Why do you think it is important not to swerve suddenly to avoid drains, potholes and parked vehicles?

_____

8–9 In the context of the passage, what does each of these words/phrases mean?

abreast (line 19)

_____

traffic calming features (lines 36–37)

_____

10–11 Explain in your own words why it is important to 'take care when overtaking'.

_____

_____

12–13 What is the difference in instruction where some rules say you '**MUST**' and others state you 'should'.

_____

_____

14–15 Is there a rule that surprises you? Why?

_____

_____

Now go to the Progress Chart to record your score!   Total   15

Add *ie* or *ei* to each of these to make a word.

1 rec____pt

2 repr____ve

3 w____r

4 perc____ve

5 y____ld

6 v____n

6

Write six words that end in a vowel other than *e*.

> Words ending in e don't count!

7–12 _____ _____ _____

_____ _____ _____

6

Add the **prefix** *aero*, *auto* or *aqua* to each of these words.

> A prefix is added to the beginning of a word.

13 dynamic _____

14 plane _____

15 graph _____

16 biography _____

17 drome _____

18 marine _____

6

Write a **homophone** for each of these words.

> A homophone has the same sound as another word but a different meaning or spelling.

19 board _____

20 higher _____

21 idle _____

22 dough _____

23 taught _____

24 sole _____

6

Add *or* or *ar* to each of these words.

25 instruct_____

26 perpendicul_____

27 simil_____

28 warri_____

29 particul_____

30 profess_____

6

There are two items of punctuation missing in each of these sentences. Write what they are and circle where they should go in the sentence.

1–2 "Im looking for my toothbrush," moaned Tim

_____   _____

3–4 "Who are you whispered Jamie.

_____   _____

5–6 She felt a cold hand touch her face chilling her to the bone

_____   _____

7–8 Without warning Nicola grabbed Najibs arm.

_____   _____

9–10 Barney, the dog came in covered with mud after his walk

_____   _____

11–12 "I'll carry it" offered Mum "It really is very heavy."

_____   _____

12

Write a short passage. Include two statements, two questions and an exclamation.

13–17 _____

_____

_____

_____

_____

_____

5

Underline the two **clauses** in each of these sentences.

Remember, a clause must have a verb.

18–19 When will this rain stop because I really want to go outside?

20–21 The lorry driver made a mess of the verge as he avoided the cyclist.

22–23 They walked along the path kicking at stones.

24–25 The plane dropped suddenly and the passengers screamed!

26–27 The vase crashed to the ground breaking into many pieces.

10

Rewrite each sentence as if you are writing about yourself.

28 She smiled at herself in the mirror.

_____

29 They dashed to the shop before it closed.

_____

30 He hurt himself as he climbed over the fence.

_____

3

> Use a different verb in each sentence.

Add a **verb** to complete these sentences.

1 Cleo, the cat, _____ the birds before she caught one.

2 Damien reluctantly _____ on his homework.

3 The family _____ to catch the train just before it pulled out of the station.

4 As time _____, the boredom set in.

5 The concert music could be _____ a great distance away.

6 Jay thinks peanuts _____ delicious.

⬤ 6

Write what type of **adverb** these words are. Write *place*, *time* or *manner* next to each one.

> Adverbs provide information on place (for example, here), time (for example, soon) or manner (for example, quickly).

7 somewhere _____

8 lovely _____

9 incredibly _____

10 away _____

11 already _____

12 easily _____

⬤ 6

Complete the following **adjectives** of comparison.

For example: slow slower slowest

13–14 easy _____ _____

15–16 cheerful _____ _____

17–18 wealthy _____ _____

19–20 beautiful _____ _____

⬤ 8

Copy these sentences, substituting a possessive **pronoun** in place of the underlined words.

21–22 Their toys are damaged and broken much more than our toys.

_____

23–24 Lucy's room is much tidier than my room.

_____

25–26 My bike goes faster free-wheeling than Luke's bike.

_____

27–28 My animals take much longer to clean than the school's animals.

_____

29–30 Tilly's jumps are higher and further than Kyle's jumps.

_____ 10

Focus test 9 | Vocabulary

Write these words in reverse **alphabetical order**.

> Hint: work out the alphabetical order, then reverse the order you write the words!

1–6   facility   factor

       fabric   fabulous

       fable   face

_____ _____ _____

_____ _____ _____

Write an **onomatopoeic** word for each of the following.

7   crisps being eaten   _____

8   water going down a plughole   _____

9   a crow call   _____

10   a coin dropping into a bucket of water   _____

11   potato being mashed   _____

12   a firework being let off   _____

Circle the words that have been 'borrowed' from other countries.

13–18   opera   house   pizza

          bungalow   chutney   horse

          tree   restaurant   chef

6

6

6

Write two **compound words** using each of these words.

A compound word is a word made up using two other words.

19 back   _____

            _____

20 eye   _____

            _____

21 fore   _____

            _____

22 hair   _____

            _____

23 motor   _____

            _____

24 sun   _____

            _____

6

Complete these **similes**.

A simile is an expression used to describe what something is like.

25 He is as cold as _____.

26 She is as graceful as a _____.

27 He swims like a _____.

28 She runs like a _____.

29 He is as sneaky as a _____.

30 She dives like a _____.

6

The Man from Snowy River

This poem is set in Australia and was written around 1890.
The poem tells the story of a horseback pursuit to recapture the colt of a
prizewinning racehorse that escaped from its paddock and is living with wild horses.

There was movement at the station, for the word had passed around
That the colt from Old Regret had got away,
And had joined the wild bush horses – he was worth a thousand pounds,
So all the cracks had gathered to the fray.
All the tried and noted riders from the stations near and far   5
Had mustered at the homestead overnight,
For the bushmen love hard riding where the wild bush horses are,
And the stock horse snuffs the battle with delight …

… – they found the horses by the big mimosa clump –
They raced away towards the mountain's brow,   10
And the old man gave his orders, "Boys, go at them from the jump,
No use to try for fancy riding now.
And, Clancy, you must wheel them, try and wheel them to the right.
Ride boldly, lad, and never fear the spills,
For never yet was rider that could keep the mob in sight,   15
If once they gain the shelter of those hills." …

When they reached the mountain's summit, even Clancy took a pull,
It well might make the boldest hold their breath,
The wild hop scrub grew thickly, and the hidden ground was full
Of wombat holes, and any slip was death.   20
But the man from Snowy River let the pony have his head,
And he swung his stock whip round and gave a cheer,
And he raced him down the mountain like a torrent down its bed,
While the others stood and watched in very fear.

He sent the flint stones flying, but the pony kept his feet,   25
He cleared the fallen timber in his stride,
And the man from Snowy River never shifted in his seat –
It was grand to see that mountain horseman ride.
Through the stringy barks and saplings, on the rough and broken ground,
Down the hillside at a racing pace he went;   30
And he never drew the bridle till he landed safe and sound,
At the bottom of that terrible descent …

And he ran them single-handed till their sides were white with foam.
He followed like a bloodhound on their track,
Till they halted cowed and beaten, then he turned their heads for home,   35
And alone and unassisted brought them back.
But his hardy mountain pony he could scarcely raise a trot,
He was blood from hip to shoulder from the spur;
But his pluck was still undaunted, and his courage fiery hot,
For never yet was mountain horse a cur …   40

A.B. 'Banjo' Paterson

Answer the questions.

1 How much was the escaped horse worth?

_____

2–3 How did the bush riders feel about the journey they were about to take? Use evidence from the extract to support your answer.

_____

_____

4 Who gave orders to the other riders?

_____

5 Why was it a problem if the horses gained 'the shelter of those hills'?

_____

6–7 Where did the riders give up the chase for the wild horses? Which rider continued following them?

_____

_____

8–10 Describe in your own words how the rider pursued the wild horses.

_____

_____

11 Copy a **simile** from the poem that describes the man from Snowy River's descent down the mountain.

_____

12–13 Using evidence from the extract, describe the condition of the man from Snowy River's pony.

_____

_____

14–15 Was the escaped horse caught? How do you think the man from Snowy River felt?

_____

_____

Martin's Mice

Humans, Martin was glad to find, didn't chase cats. The farmer paid little attention to him, but the farmer's wife made sure he had enough to eat, and the farmer's daughter actually made quite a fuss of him, picking him up and cuddling him.

One day she took Martin to see her rabbits; three white rabbits with pink 5
eyes, that she kept in three large hutches at the bottom of the garden. Why did she keep them, he wondered?

The next time that Martin met his mother on his journeys, he asked her about this.

"Mother," he said. "Why does that girl keep those rabbits?" 10

"As pets," Dulcie Maude said.

"What's a pet?"

"A pet is an animal that humans keep because they like it. They like looking after it, feeding it, stroking it, making a fuss of it,"

"So we're pets, are we?" 15

"Strictly speaking, I suppose. Dogs certainly are, always fussing around humans, sucking up to them."

"What about cows and pigs and sheep?"

"No, they're not pets," said Dulcie Maude. "Humans eat them, you see."

"But they don't eat cats and dogs?" 20

"Of course not."

"And they don't eat rabbits?"

"Yes, they eat rabbits. But not *pet* rabbits."

"Why not?"

As with most mothers, there was a limit to Dulcie Maude's patience. 25

"Oh, stop your endless questions, Martin, do!" she snapped. "Curiosity, in case you don't know, killed the cat!" and she stalked off, swishing her tail.

It was curiosity, nevertheless, that led Martin to climb up the steep steps into the cart-shed loft to see what was in it. What was in it, in fact, was a load of junk. The farmer never threw anything away, in case it should come 30
in useful one day, and the loft was filled with boxes of this and bags of that, with broken tools and disused harnesses and worn-out coats and empty tins and bottles that had once contained sheep-dip or cow-drench or horse-liniment.

Against one wall stood an old white-enamelled bath with big brass taps 35
and clawed cast-iron feet, and it was while Martin was exploring beneath it that something suddenly shot out.

Automatically, he put his paw on it.

"I'm most awfully sorry!" he said again, but the fat mouse only continued to say "Mercy! Mercy!" in a quavery voice. It seemed to be rooted to 40
the spot, and it stared up at Martin with its round black eyes as though hypnotized.

How pretty it looks, thought Martin. What a dear little thing!

"Don't be frightened," he said.

"It is not for myself alone that I beg you to spare me," said the mouse. 45
"You see, I am pregnant."

What a strange name, thought Martin. I've never heard anyone called that before.

"How do you do?" he said. "I am Martin."

What a dear little thing, he thought again. I'd like to look after it, to feed it, 50
to stroke it, to make a fuss of it, just as Mother said that humans like to do with their pets.

After all, he thought, some humans eat rabbits but some keep them as pets. So, in the same way, some cats eat mice, but some…

"Shall I tell you what I am going to do with you?" he said. 55

"I know what you are going to do," said the mouse wearily. "After you've finished tormenting me, you're going to eat me."

"You're wrong," said Martin.

He bent his head and gently picked up the mouse in his mouth. Then he looked about him. Then he climbed on to an old wooden chest that stood 60
handily beside the bath and looked down into its depths.

The perfect place, he thought excitedly. My little mouse can't escape – the plug's still in the plug-hole and the sides are much too steep and slippery – but I can jump in and out easily. He jumped in and laid his burden carefully down. 65

The mouse lay motionless. Its eyes were shut, its ears drooped, its coat was wet from the kitten's mouth.

"Shall I tell you what I'm going to do?" said Martin again.

"Kill me," said the mouse feebly. "Kill me and have done."

"Not on your life!" said Martin. "I'm going to keep you for a pet!" 70

The mouse did not reply. It lay on the rust-stained bottom of the bath, shivering.

"Oh dear, you're cold!" said Martin, and he began to lick the mouse with his warm tongue. But this only made it shudder more violently, so he leaped out of the bath and began to look about the loft for something that would 75
serve as bedding for his new pet.

From *Martin's Mice* by Dick King-Smith

Answer these questions.

1 Which human paid Martin the most attention?

_____

2-3 Why, according to Dulcie Maude, did the farmer's daughter keep rabbits?

_____

_____

4–5 What does Dulcie Maude think of dogs? Why? Find evidence in the extract to support your answer.

_____

_____

6–7 Find a proverb between the lines 25 and 30. What does this proverb mean?

_____

_____

8 What did the farmer use the cart-shed loft for?

_____

_____

9 When did Martin discover the mouse?

_____

10 What type of animal is Martin?

_____

11 Describe what is meant by 'Automatically, he put a paw on it.' (line 38).

_____

_____

12 The author states that the mouse is 'rooted to the spot'. What is meant by this?

_____

_____

13 Why does Martin think the mouse has a strange name?

_____

_____

14–15 In the context of the passage, what does each of these words mean?

   a tormenting (line 57) _____

   b burden (line 64) _____

Answers will vary for questions that require the child to answer in their own words. Possible answers to most of these questions are given in *italics*.

Focus test 1: Spelling

1 scarves	2 reefs
3 photos	4 crocuses
5 diagnoses	6 muffs
7 p	8 t
9 e	10 b
11 n	12 d
13 bumped	14 shipping
15 trekked	16 knotted
17 croaking	18 whipped

19–24 necessary, science, confidence, decision, tolerance, exercise

25 elegant	26 harass
27 fulfilled	28 comparison
29 vicious	30 parliament

Focus test 2: Sentences

1 present	2 past
3 past	4 present
5 past	6 present

7–8 The children ate the cake, the biscuits, the crisps but not the sandwiches!

9 The Johnson family travelled to Auckland, New Zealand and then returned to Australia.

10–11 Jess loved the books *Coraline*, *The Secret Garden*, *The Growing Summer* and *The Silver Sword*.

12 Where have I put my blue goggles that let the water in, my stripy swimsuit and beach towel that has a mark on it?

13 W J Hardiman

14 Hong Kong

15 *A Small Pinch of Weather*

16 Mrs Zucherman

17 *American Indian Myths and Legends*

18 *Harry Potter and the Philosopher's Stone*

19–23 "It is freezing outside," complained Jake. "I need my gloves."

24 o'clock	25 could've
26 they'll	27 don't
28 there's	29 we're
30 shan't	

Focus test 3: Grammar

1 grab	2 slice
3 tear	4 gobble
5 scrub	6 smash

7–14

Proper nouns	Abstract nouns	Common nouns	Collective nouns
Kuwait	hate	axe	colony
Doughton	love	pen pal	host

15–16 Andy climbed <u>over</u> the gate <u>into</u> the field of cows.

17 The hat was blown <u>off</u> his head as the wind gusted.

18 The cat jumped <u>onto</u> the wall to survey her territory.

19 Frankie was sitting <u>in</u> the study doing her homework.

20–21 <u>Beyond</u> the fields, the sun could be seen glinting <u>through</u> the clouds.

22 *Child's sentence with an adverb underlined. E.g. The dog <u>happily</u> chased the ball.*

23 *Child's sentence with an adjective underlined. E.g. The boy flew the <u>red</u> kite.*

24 *Child's sentence with a pronoun underlined. E.g. Did <u>he</u> really want that?*

25 *Child's sentence with a verb underlined. E.g. The wheels of the car <u>skidded</u> on the ice.*

26 *Child's sentence with a connective underlined. E.g. The film was great <u>but</u> it was a bit too long.*

27 The <u>freezing cold, bleak</u> weather encouraged the children to stay indoors.

28 The <u>healthy, red-faced, old</u> gentleman danced through the night.

29 The <u>fast-paced, exciting</u> game lasted for hours.

30 The <u>wet, slimy, stinking</u> mud clung to their boots.

Focus test 4: Vocabulary

1 hen	2 duchess
3 grandmother	4 mare
5 doe	6 bride
7 *never*	8 *question/query*
9 *natural*	10 *descend*
11 *inaccurate*	12 *deny*

13 *tiredness resulting from hard work*

14 *unclear, not clearly expressed*

15 *a conversation or discussion*

Bond STRETCH English Tests and Papers 9–10 years

16 *a place of worship for Jewish people*
17 *a long speech by one performer*
18 *an introduction to something*

19 maths	**20** paper
21 phone	**22** ad or advert
23 intro	**24** net

25 All good things come to an end.
26 Barking up the wrong tree.
27 The boot is on the other foot.
28 Rub salt in the wound.
29 Keep your shirt on.
30 As snug as a bug in a rug.

Focus test 5: Comprehension 1

1 You should wear reflective clothing or accessories once it gets dark (and always a helmet).

2–3 Cycling clothes shouldn't be loose or flap around as they may get caught in the chainwheel or cover the lights. Light-coloured or fluorescent clothes will also help you to be seen. A helmet should always be worn.

4 Amber pedal reflectors were introduced on 1 October 1985.

5–6 Rule 66 states 'be considerate of other road users, particularly blind and partially sighted pedestrians'.

7 It is dangerous to swerve while cycling as there are other road users and they won't expect you to suddenly move out into the road and therefore could knock into you.

8–9 Abreast (line 19) means side by side, in the same direction.
Traffic calming features (lines 36–37) means additions made to the road that are intended to slow the traffic.

10–11 *Child to consider all the dangers that they need to be aware of when overtaking, for example know what is behind them, be aware of the speed vehicles are travelling around them, and other potential dangers, for instance cars pulling out of side roads.*

12–13 The difference between a '**MUST**' and a 'should' instruction is that a '**MUST**' instruction has to be obeyed but a 'should' instruction suggests that it would be a good idea to do something but it isn't absolutely essential.

14–15 *Child's own answer highlighting a rule that they find surprising and why (or if they do not find any surprising, why not).*

Focus test 6: Spelling

1 receipt	**2** reprieve
3 weir	**4** perceive
5 yield	**6** vein

7–12 *piano, spaghetti, viola, cello, pizza, volcano*

13 aerodynamic	
14 aeroplane or aquaplane	
15 autograph	**16** autobiography
17 aerodrome	**18** aquamarine
19 bored	**20** hire
21 idol	**22** doe
23 taut/torte	**24** soul
25 instructor	**26** perpendicular
27 similar	**28** warrior
29 particular	**30** professor

Focus test 7: Sentences

1–2 "I'm looking for my toothbrush," moaned Tim.
3–4 "Who are you**?**" whispered Jamie.
5–6 She felt a cold hand touch her face, chilling her to the bone.
7–8 Without warning, Nicola grabbed Najib's arm.
9–10 Barney, the dog, came in covered with mud after his walk.
11–12 "I'll carry it," offered Mum. "It really is very heavy."
13–17 *Child's own passage including two statements, two questions and an exclamation, punctuated correctly.*
18–19 When will this rain stop because I really want to go outside?
20–21 The lorry driver made a mess of the verge as he avoided the cyclist.
22–23 They walked along the path kicking at stones.
24–25 The plane dropped suddenly and the passengers screamed!
26–27 The vase crashed to the ground breaking into many pieces.
28 I smiled at myself in the mirror.
29 I dashed to the shop before it closed.
30 I hurt myself as I climbed over the fence.

Focus test 8: Grammar

1 Cleo, the cat, *watched* the birds before she caught one.
2 Damien reluctantly *worked* on his homework.
3 The family *rushed* to catch the train just before it pulled out of the station.
4 As time *passed,* the boredom set in.
5 The concert music could be *heard* a great distance away.
6 Jay thinks peanuts *taste* delicious.
7 place
8 manner
9 manner
10 place
11 time
12 manner
13–14 easier, easiest
15–16 more cheerful, most cheerful
17–18 wealthier, wealthiest
19–20 more beautiful, most beautiful
21–22 Theirs are damaged and broken much more than ours.
23–24 Hers is much tidier than mine.
25–26 Mine goes faster free-wheeling than his.
27–28 Mine take much longer to clean than theirs.
29–30 Hers are higher and further than his.

Focus test 9: Vocabulary

1 factor
2 facility
3 face
4 fabulous
5 fabric
6 fable
7 *crunch*
8 *glug*
9 *squawk*
10 *plop*
11 *squelch*
12 *whizz*
13–18 opera, pizza, bungalow, chutney, restaurant, chef
19 *backstroke, backwater*
20 *eyelash, eyewitness*
21 *forethought, forearm*
22 *hairspray, hairpin*
23 *motorboat, motorcycle*
24 *sundown, sunflower*
25 *He is as cold as ice.*
26 *She is as graceful as a swan.*
27 *He swims like a fish.*
28 *She runs like a cheetah.*
29 *He is as sneaky as a fox.*
30 *She dives like a dolphin.*

Focus test 10: Comprehension 2

1 The escaped horse was worth a thousand pounds.
2–3 The bush riders were excited and ready for the ride, 'For the bushmen love hard riding where the wild bush horses are'.
4 The old man gave the orders to the other riders.
5 The hills provided shelter in the form of a thick scrub. The riding was much more dangerous for those on horseback.
6–7 The riders stopped at the top of the mountain. The man from Snowy River didn't hesitate when chasing the wild horses down the mountain side.
8–10 *Child's own answer describing how the man from Snowy River pursued the horses without fear, with excitement, at great speed and with great skill.*
11 The simile 'he raced him down the mountain like a torrent down its bed' describes the descent down the mountain.
12–13 *Child's own answer to make reference to the fact that the pony was exhausted, barely being able to trot, 'he could scarcely raise a trot' (line 37), he was bleeding where he had been driven on by his rider, 'blood from hip to shoulder' (line 38) but he had loved the ride.*
14–15 Yes, the escaped horse was caught, as this line describes, 'Till they halted cowed and beaten, then he turned their heads for home'. The man from Snowy River must have felt exhausted but elated, achieving what he had.

Bond STRETCH English Tests and Papers 9–10 years

1 The farmer's daughter made quite a fuss of Martin.

2–3 The farmer's daughter kept rabbits as pets because she liked them and liked looking after them.

4–5 Dulcie Maude has a low opinion of dogs, suggesting that they ask for attention from humans, as the sentence, 'always fussing around humans, sucking up to them' indicates.

6–7 'Curiosity killed the cat' (lines 26–27) is a proverb. It means beware of the dangers of unnecessary investigation.

8 The farmer used the cart-shed loft for storing everything he thought might be useful one day.

9 Martin discovered the mouse as it shot out from under the bath while he was exploring the cart-shed loft.

10 Martin is a cat/kitten.

11 The word 'automatically' has been used in the sentence as it is an instinct for cats to catch mice.

12 If you are 'rooted to the spot', this implies that you can't move because anything growing with roots can't move on its own.

13 Martin thinks the mouse has a strange name because he thinks it is called 'pregnant' and he hasn't heard the word before.

14–15 a Tormenting (line 57) means teasing or provoking.
b Burden (line 64) means something carried or a heavy load.

16–18 You can tell that the mouse felt terrified during its encounter with Martin by the following extracts: "I beg you to spare me" (line 45), "Kill me and have done" (line 69) and "made it shudder more violently" (line 74).

19–20 Martin might want to keep his mouse a secret because Dulcie Maude might laugh at him or, worse still, might eat his pet!

21 *learn*
22 *worm*
23 *route*
24 *laugh*
25 *bough*

26 separate
27 interrupt
28 persistence
29 medieval
30 noticeable
31 more expensive
32 sillier
33 better
34 happier
35 more beautiful
36 impolite
37 unreliable
38 illegitimate
39 impatient
40 illiterate
41 noun
42 verb
43 verb
44 noun
45 noun
46 *I don't want any help.*
47 *We aren't ever going to get there.*
48 *There isn't a toilet in this shop.*
49 *The sun is never going to come out today.*
50 *We have got no money.*
51 *sweaty* runner
52 *glossy* vase
53 *henpecked* chicken
54 *dog-eared* book
55 *delicious* chips
56 Their
57 his
58 She
59 they
60 it
61–65 miniskirt, hillock, figurine, eaglet, gosling
66 a type of vegetable   okra
67 a person who works on machinery   machinist
68 something that follows on from an earlier event   sequel
69 a disadvantage   drawback
70 small fragments   smithereens
71–75 *Five compound words using the word 'back', for example, backstroke, backdrop, backbite, backtrack, backlash, backhand.*
76 *Something good that isn't recognised initially.*

77 Con____ _g to be upset about something that happened in the past._

78 _People cannot fundamentally alter their main characteristics._

79 _A small, mild punishment._

80 _When something that isn't nice happens to you after you have mistreated others._

81–85 Niall was enjoying a cycle ride when suddenly a car swerved towards him. "Watch out!" he screamed, but he was too late. "Where am I?" was his first question as he came around after the accident.

full stop = 3
exclamation mark = 1
question mark = 1

86–90 _Child's own sentences using the connectives correctly. A connective is a word (or words) that joins clauses or sentences._

91 Harry (is or was) hurt after falling off the shed roof.

92 We (are or were) going to have a barbeque despite the fact it (is or was) raining!

93 The birds (were) singing happily until the cat came along.

94 The sea (is or was) freezing but we still (are or were) going in for a swim!

95 might not

96 what will

97 must have

98 how will

99–100 why is, why has

Mixed paper 2

1 Most Victorian factory owners' main concern was to make money.

2 Despite poor working conditions, there were always people who needed a job.

3 Laws were introduced to protect workers.

4 Children would have been chosen as they were small and could get under and between the pieces of machinery to clean them.

5–6 Working under machinery was very dangerous as hair or clothes could be caught, causing horrific injuries. In 1884 a law was passed to protect moving parts of machinery in cotton mills, though it took a long time until this was enforced.

7–9 _Child's own answer detailing life as a child in a factory. Information needs to be included about long hours, tiredness and rough treatment._

10–11 _Child's own opinion, for example, 'The punishments were effective up to a point, but the factory owners could have shown workers that if they worked hard, they would improve their working conditions.'_

12 The overseer was in charge of the factory floor. He supervised the workers.

13 Phosphorus is a chemical that was used to make matches.

14–15 The workers were given no compensation for either having a day off or for becoming ill as a result of their terrible working conditions. There was always the potential that they might lose their job.

16 If they didn't have family to support them, they would end up at the workhouse.

17–18 In 1895 workers began to be given compensation for industrial illness.

19–20 _Child's own answer stating what they think needs improving most urgently and why._

21 reversible

22 infusing

23 refusal

24 operator

25 largest

26–30

Verb	Past tense	Present tense
to grab	grabbed	grab/grabs
to watch	watched	watch/watches
to glide	glided	glide/glides
to munch	munched	munch/munches

31 circum **32** bi

33 trans **34** tele

35 auto

36–40 suddenly, questionnaire, immediate, familiar, occurrence

41 The rabbit loved to eat its carrot.

42 The party continued into the evening.

43 I ate a snack before lunch.

44 Dennis painted a/the wall many times.

45 The pencil was broken by the child.

46 caught

47 find

48 loves

Bond STRETCH English Tests and Papers 9–10 years

49 blew

50 squeezed

51 hers

52 mine

53 yours

54 his

55 ours

56 soon

57 behind

58 next

59 failure

60 exciting

61–65 *Child's own pairs of gender words, for example, duke – duchess, uncle – aunt, dog – bitch.*

66–70 puppet, purchase, purify, purist, purse

71 JP

72 USA

73 kg

74 VIP

75 PTO

76–80 worm, purple, year, dandelion, phone

81–89 **O**verlooking the **M**artha **B**rae **R**iver is the **G**ood **H**ope **G**reat **H**ouse, a fine example of a **G**eorgian house**,** furnished with antiques and with a commanding view of the surrounding countryside. **T**ours are available around the house and estate**,** with its old water wheel**,** kiln and sugar mill ruins.

90 the dog's lead

91 the firefighters' helmets

92 the kangaroos' pouches

93 the horses' saddles

94 the children's classroom

95 the girl's shoe

96–100 *The child's sentences, each with a further clause added. A clause is a section of a sentence with a verb.*

Mixed paper 3

1 James Reeves describes the sea as a hungry dog.

2–3 The lines describe the sea coming in and out, up and down the beach, moving the stones as it does so.

4 It describes a quiet, windless day when even the reeds next to the shore no longer make a sound.

5–6 The second verse describes a rough and wild sea. The line, 'Shaking his wet sides over the cliffs,' illustrates a rough, wild sea as it is describing the sea spray crashing against the cliffs.

7 The sea is barely moving, it is calm and tranquil.

8–9 *Child's own answer stating whether they like the link James Reeves makes with a hungry sea dog in his poem and why.*

10–11 *Child's description of the sea, touching on the different aspects that are described in the first verse of 'The Sea'.*

12–13 Yes, the way he describes the sea is full of warmth and interest.

14 A tall ship is referred to in the poem 'Sea Fever'.

15 The wind is like a sharp knife, it is a strong, cold wind.

16–17 It is likely that 'Sea Fever' has been written first as the language used is from an earlier period, for example 'whetted', 'yarn'.

18 The poet would like to go with company as the line 'And all I ask is a merry yarn from a laughing fellow-rover,' suggests.

19–20 *Child's answer detailing which poem they liked the best and why.*

21–25 merciful, hopeful, bountiful, doubtful, dutiful

26 countries

27 lilies

28 buoys

29 flies

30 valleys

31 conceit

32 retrieve

33 hygiene

34 deceive

35 belief

36 *announcement*

37 *scarceness*

38 *likely*

39 *spaceship*

40 *motherhood*

41–46

Concrete nouns	Abstract nouns
kite	excitement
sky	terror
ground	relief

47 *Mum suggested that it was time to get ready.*

48 *Daniel asked where they were going tomorrow.*

49 *Jay questioned whether he had to go to school today.*

50 *Dad had an idea and suggested they go on a bike ride.*

51–55 *Five prepositions (a word that relates other words to each other) listed, for example above, among, past, beside, within.*

56–60

Adjectives	Comparative adjectives	Superlative adjectives
heavy	heavier	heaviest
good	better	best
stupid	more stupid	most stupid

61 important, distinguished

62 something that is about to happen

63 to make sure

64 to take out insurance

65 past tense of 'to buy'

66 past tense of 'to bring'

67 France

68 Italy

69 France

70 Italy

71 Germany

72–75 *plop, drip, splash, splosh*

76–80 *odd, unfamiliar, weird, crazy, peculiar*

81–84 "I can't do this anymore!" screamed Leah, as she buried her head in her numeracy homework.

85–91 Tyler asked, "What time is the clown arriving?" "Quarter to four," replied his mum.
(1 mark is also given for the new line when a different person begins speaking.)

92–95 Towan Beach, a private beach with perfect sand, is set behind the Trewince Manor Hotel, just a mile from Portscatho.

96–100 *The given sentences completed with phrases. A phrase is a group of words that usually doesn't contain a subject or a verb.*

Mixed paper 4

1 Jung Chang was six when she started primary school.

2 'Major occupation' is the way Jung Chang describes her role of picking up steel items. Like a job, it occupies her time.

3–5 *Child's own description of Jung Chang's walk to school, describing how long it takes, what the scenery is like, what she does on the way.*

6–8 *Child's answer describing the difference between their own school life and that of Jung Chang's, for example the role of the teacher, the number of lessons, the role of the student.*

9–10 a 'Preoccupied' means engaged.
b 'Frantically' means agitated and anxious.

11 We know the furnaces are dangerous as Jung Chang visited a teacher in hospital who had been burned by the molten iron.

12–13 The most shocking information in paragraph two is the fact that nurses were actually feeding the furnaces through operations, rather than concentrating on the operations that were being performed.

14 Jung Chang moved to a special compound, the centre of government for the province.

15 They now had to eat in a canteen, they no longer had to prepare their own food.

16 Jung Chang's parents were sometimes expected to keep the furnace's temperature in their office up so it never dropped.

17–18 If the labour force were no longer working on the land, they were not producing the food needed to feed people. Therefore, there wouldn't be enough food and people would start to starve.

19–20 *Child's answer showing they can empathise with the people of China at this time.*

21 extraordinary

22 contradictory

23 battery

24 satisfactory

25 delivery

26 bred

27 chews

28 hoarse

29 mousse

30 wrung

31 banjo

32 buffalo

33 cocoa

34 vitamin

35 drama

36 hoof

37 wolf

38 fishwife

39 penknife

40 wharf

41–45 *Five sentences that include each of the listed adverbs.*

46–47 *happiness, sadness*

48–49 *its, their*

50–51 *because, therefore*

52–53 *largest, smallest*

54–55 *drag, scream*

56–60 *Child's own examples of adjectival phrases using the nouns given. An adjectival phrase is a group of words that describes a noun.*

61 foreign

62 depend

63 incident

64 acquaint

65 doubt

66 to suffer from deafness

67 to keep silent

68 to rain very heavily

69 to be sleepy

70 to be someone very special

71 abbreviation

72 Before Christ

73 adjective

74 volume

75 number

76–77 *mean, spiteful*

78–80 *rough, uneven, bumpy*

81–100 It was a hot morning. Mum opened Jacob's curtains before turning to him. "Today is a special day. Get up quickly!" and she left. Five minutes later he was having his breakfast. "I am impressed," stated Mum, "I wish you were this quick every day!"
"Where are we off to?" asked Jacob.
"Nowhere ... but we've a visitor," she smiled.

16–18 The mouse felt terrified during the encounter with Martin. Use evidence from the extract to support this statement.

_____

_____

_____

19–20 Why might Martin want to keep his new pet a secret from Dulcie Maude?

_____

_____

_____

○ 20

Write a word with the same letter string as the example but with a different pronunciation.
For example: rew<u>ard</u>   g<u>ard</u>en

21 b<u>ear</u>   _____   22 p<u>or</u>trait   _____

23 c<u>oul</u>d   _____   24 t<u>au</u>ght   _____

25 th<u>ough</u>t   _____

○ 5

All these words have been spelled incorrectly.
Rewrite the words, spelling them correctly.

26 seperate   _____   27 interupt   _____

28 persistance   _____   29 medeival   _____

30 noticable   _____

○ 5

Write a **comparative** for each of these words.

31 expensive   _____   32 silly   _____

33 good   _____   34 happy   _____

35 beautiful   _____

○ 5

Add the **prefix** _un_, _im_ or _il_ to make a word.

36 _____polite   37 _____reliable

38 _____legitimate   39 _____patient

40 _____literate

○ 5

25

Write whether each word is a **noun** or a **verb**.

41 conclusion _____   42 explain _____

43 compete _____   44 definition _____

45 reflection _____

5

Rewrite these sentences without the double negatives.

46 I don't want no help.

_____

47 We aren't never going to get there.

_____

48 There isn't no toilet in this shop.

_____

49 The sun isn't never going to come out today.

_____

50 We haven't got no money.

_____

5

Add an interesting **adjective** to each of these nouns.

51 _____ runner   52 _____ vase

53 _____ chicken   54 _____ book

55 _____ chips

5

Substitute each of the underlined words for a **pronoun**.

56 The boys' scooters were parked outside the house. _____

57 Meg kicked Jacob's football over the wall. _____

58 Leah is a great hairdresser. _____

59 Where have Meena and Kelly gone? _____

60 Have you collected the birthday cake yet? _____

5

Circle the **diminutives**.

61–65 kitchen   miniskirt   hillock

          jumper   figurine   fence

          eaglet   gosling   thunder

With a line, match the **definitions** to the correct words.

66 a type of vegetable   machinist

67 a person who works on machinery   sequel

68 something that follows on from an earlier event   drawback

69 a disadvantage   smithereens

70 small fragments   okra

Write five **compound words**. Each compound word must use the word *back*.

71–75 _____   _____   _____

          _____   _____

In your own words, describe what each of these **idioms** mean.

76 a blessing in disguise

_____

77 a chip on your shoulder

_____

78 a leopard cannot change its spots

_____

79 a slap on the wrist

_____

80 a taste of your own medicine

_____

Read this short passage. The full stops, exclamation marks and question marks are missing. How many of each are missing?

81–85 Niall was enjoying a cycle ride, when suddenly a car swerved towards him "Watch out" he screamed, but he was too late "Where am I" was his first question as he came around after the accident

full stop	=	☐
exclamation mark	=	☐
question mark	=	☐

5

Write each of these **connectives** into your own sentences.

86 however   _____

87 therefore   _____

88 yet   _____

89 besides   _____

90 consequently _____

5

Add *is*, *are*, *was* or *were* to each gap to complete the sentence correctly. There can be more than one correct answer.

91 Harry _____ hurt after falling off the shed roof.

92 We _____ going to have a barbeque despite the fact that it

_____ raining!

93 The birds _____ singing happily until the cat came along.

94 The sea _____ freezing but we still _____ going in for a swim!

4

Write the full form of each of these **contracted** words.

95 mightn't   _____   **96** what'll   _____

97 must've   _____   **98** how'll   _____

99–100 why's   _____

_____

6

Dangers in a Victorian Factory

Early factory work was unhealthy and dangerous as were many other
Victorian jobs. The only concern of most factory owners was making money.
They did not worry about the health and safety of their workers. There were
always many people willing to work in the factories, even if the conditions
were poor. Until laws were made to protect workers, the owners were not   5
forced to think about safety.

Safety at work

Children were often found under the huge items of machinery. They
had to clean fluff away from the machinery while it was still running. This
could be very dangerous. Imagine what would happen if workers caught   10
their hair or clothes in the machinery while they were working or leaning
over it.
In 1884 a law was passed to force cotton mill owners to put guards over
the moving parts of some of their machinery, but it was not until much
later that all factories had to protect their workers in this way.   15

Punishment

Children were often so tired from working long hours that they could not
work quickly or concentrate. Men in charge of the children kept them
at work by shouting at them or punishing them. A beating was quite
a common event in some factories. A few overseers were very cruel.   20
For example, a common punishment in one nail-making factory in the
Midlands was to drive a nail through the worker's ear into the wooden
bench. There were no laws to protect children against such cruelty.

Chemical danger

Workers often had to use dangerous chemicals in their work. For   25
example, phosphorus was used to make matches. Its fumes could
damage a matchworker's bones. Phosphorus made teeth drop out and
even jaws rot away. Until the later part of the Victorian period, there were
no laws to punish employers for unhealthy working conditions.

Working conditions

Factories could be very crowded and very noisy. There were no rules about how many people could work in one factory, or whether there was too much noise from the factory machinery.

In a Victorian factory, workers would spend hours in a noisy, crowded room with poor lighting. The atmosphere could be stuffy in summer or cold with no heating in winter.

Industrial illnesses

If people became ill at work, their family or friends took them home. There were no doctors or nurses working, even in the largest factories. Workers weren't given any money as compensation by the factory owners if their illnesses or injuries were caused by bad working conditions. In fact, workers who missed a day's work, missed a day's pay. Workers who could no longer work ended up in the workhouse, unless their family could support them and look after them. It was only after 1895 that some workers were given compensation for industrial illness.

Adapted from *A Victorian Factory* by Lyn Gash and Sheila Watson

Answer these questions.

1 What was the main concern of most Victorian factory owners?

_____

2 Write in your own words what is meant by the sentence, 'There were always many people willing to work in the factories, even if the conditions were poor.' (lines 4–5)

_____

3 What made the factory owners first think about safety in their factories?

_____

4 Why do you think that children were chosen to work under machinery?

_____

5–6 What could be the result of working under machinery? When did things start to improve?

_____

_____

7–9 Describe in your own words what life would be like as a child factory worker.
Use evidence from the extract to support your answer.

_____

_____

_____

10–11 Do you think that the punishments used were effective? What else could the factory owner have done instead?

_____

_____

_____

12 Explain the role of the 'overseer'.

_____

13 What is phosphorus and what was it used for?

_____

14–15 Why was illness a big concern for factory workers?

_____

_____

_____

16 What happened to workers who could no longer work?

_____

17–18 When, and in what form, did things begin to improve for ill factory workers?

_____

_____

19–20 In your opinion, which condition within the Victorian factory would need improving on behalf of the factory workers most urgently. Why?

_____

_____

_____

20

Complete these word sums.

21 reverse + ible = _____

22 infuse + ing = _____

23 refuse + al = _____

24 operate + or = _____

25 large + est = _____

5

Fill the missing gaps in the table.

26–30

Verb	Past tense	Present tense
to grab	grabbed	
to watch		
to glide		glide/glides
to munch		munch/munches

5

Write the **prefix** used in each of these words.

31 circumnavigate   prefix = _____

32 biannual   prefix = _____

33 transatlantic   prefix = _____

34 television   prefix = _____

35 autocue   prefix = _____

5

Circle the words spelled incorrectly.

36–40

important	suddnly	questionaire
exaggerate	burglary	imediate
familar	perpendicular	signature
cooperate	ocurrence	adorable

5

Rewrite these sentences, changing them from **plural** to **singular**.

41 The rabbits loved to eat their carrots.

_____

42 The parties continued into the evening.

_____

43 I ate many snacks before lunch.

_____

44 Dennis painted some walls many times.

_____

45 The pencils were broken by the children.

_____ ⬭ 5

Circle the correct form of the **verb** to complete each sentence.

46 The gang catched/caught the escaped dog.

47 The teacher can't find/found her red pen.

48 Doris loves/love to make cupcakes.

49 The wind blow/blew the slide over and broke it.

50 A mouse squeezing/squeezed into a crack in the wall. ⬭ 5

Write the possessive **pronoun** found in each of these sentences.

51 I want hers. _____

52 Is that mine? _____

53 Don't forget yours! _____

54 His is faster. _____

55 Ours looks huge. _____ ⬭ 5

Match each of these words to their word class.

behind   exciting   failure   next   soon

56 an adverb _____

57 a preposition _____

58 a connective _____

59 a noun _____

60 an adjective _____ ⬭ 5

Write five pairs of gender words.
For example: prince – princess

61 _____ – _____

62 _____ – _____

63 _____ – _____

64 _____ – _____

65 _____ – _____

⟨ 5 ⟩

Put these words in **alphabetical order**.

66–70 purify   purse   puppet   purist   purchase

_____   _____

_____   _____

_____

⟨ 5 ⟩

Copy the sentences and abbreviate the words that can be abbreviated in the sentences.

71 The Justice of the Peace ordered a prison sentence of six years.

_____

72 During the Olympic Games the United States of America swimming team won nine gold medals.

_____

73 Hannah bought 1 kilogram of apples.

_____

74 The very important person was shown to his seat.

_____

75 Please turn over.

_____

⟨ 5 ⟩

Circle the words that do not have an **antonym**.

76–80 tight   worm   child   purple   year

sit   messy   dandelion   phone

⟨ 5 ⟩

34

Rewrite this short passage, adding the missing capital letters and commas.

81–89 overlooking the martha brae river is the good hope great house a fine example of a georgian house furnished with antiques and with a commanding view of the surrounding countryside. tours are available around the house and estate with its old water wheel kiln and sugar mill ruins.

_____

_____

_____

_____

⬭ 9

Rewrite the **phrases** correctly, adding the missing apostrophes.

90 the dogs lead _____

91 the firefighters helmets _____

92 the kangaroos pouches _____

93 the horses saddles _____

94 the childrens classroom _____

95 the girls shoe _____

⬭ 6

Write a second **clause** to extend each of these sentences.

96 The car finally cut out _____

_____

97 It is the hottest day of the year so far _____

_____

98 The sheep escaped _____

_____

99 My mobile phone never works _____

_____

100 Many people entered the road safety competition _____

_____

⬭ 5

Now go to the Progress Chart to record your score!   Total ⬭ 100

(35)

The Sea

The sea is a hungry dog,
Giant and grey.
He rolls on the beach all day.
With his clashing teeth and shaggy jaws
Hour upon hour he gnaws   5
The rumbling, tumbling stones,
And "Bones, bones, bones, bones!"
The giant sea-dog moans.
Licking his greasy paws.

And when the night wind roars   10
And the moon rocks in the stormy cloud,
He bounds to his feet and snuffs and sniffs,
Shaking his wet sides over the cliffs,
And howls and hollos long and loud.

But on quiet days in May or June,   15
When even the grasses on the dune
Play no more their reedy tune,
With his head between his paws
He lies on the sandy shores,
So quiet, so quiet, he scarcely snores.   20

James Reeves

Sea Fever

I must go down to the seas again, to the lonely sea and the sky,
And all I ask is a tall ship and a star to steer her by;
And the wheel's kick and the wind's song and the white sail's shaking,
And a grey mist on the sea's face, and a grey dawn breaking.

I must go down to the seas again, for the call of the running tide   5
Is a wild call and a clear call that may not be denied;
And all I ask is a windy day with the white clouds flying,
And the flung spray and the blown spume, and the sea-gulls crying.

I must go down to the seas again, to the vagrant gypsy life,
To the gull's way and the whale's way, where the wind's like a whetted   10
knife;
And all I ask is a merry yarn from a laughing fellow-rover,
And quiet sleep and a sweet dream when the long trick's over.

John Masefield

Answer these questions.

1 What does James Reeves describe the sea as, in his poem 'The Sea'?

_____

2–3 What are the following (lines 5–6) from 'The Sea' describing?
'Hour upon hour he gnaws
The rumbling, tumbling stones,'

_____

_____

4 What is meant by the line, 'Play no more their reedy tune,' (line 17) in the poem 'The Sea'?

_____

5–6 Which verse in the poem 'The Sea' describes a rough, wild sea? Choose a line that illustrates this.

_____

_____

7 In the poem 'The Sea' what is the sea doing in the lines,
'With his head between his paws
He lies on the sandy shores'

_____

8–9 Do you like the way James Reeves has likened the sea to an animal? Why?

_____

_____

10–11 In your own words, describe the sea as found in the first verse of 'The Sea'.

_____

_____

12–13 Does John Masefield give you the impression that he likes the sea? Why?

_____

_____

14 What type of boat is referred to in 'Sea Fever'?

_____

15 What does the phrase 'the wind is like a whetted knife' (lines 10–11) mean in the poem 'Sea Fever'?

_____

16–17 Read both the poems again. Which do you think might have been written first? Why?

_____

_____

18 Does the poet in 'Sea Fever' want to go to the sea alone or with some company?

_____

19–20 Which of the two poems do you prefer. Explain why.

_____

_____

_____

20

Which of these words can have the **suffix** *ful* added to them?
Write the words with the suffix.

21–25 mercy   hope   bounty   trek

special   doubt   duty   satisfy

_____   _____   _____

_____   _____

5

Write these words in their **plural** form.

26 country   _____   **27** lily   _____

28 buoy   _____   **29** fly   _____

30 valley   _____

5

Complete these words with *ie* or *ei*.

31 conc __ __ t   32 retr __ __ ve

33 hyg __ __ ne   34 dec __ __ ve

35 bel __ __ f

5

Add a **suffix** that begins with a consonant, to each of these words.

36 announce _____   37 scarce   _____

38 like   _____   39 space   _____

40 mother   _____

5

Complete the table with **nouns** found in this short passage.

41–46 The kite sped through the sky. Jenny felt excitement as it swooped around but terror as it nearly hit her! Relief swept through her as it crashed to the ground.

Concrete nouns	Abstract nouns

6

Change these sentences from direct speech into reported speech.

47 "It is time to get ready," suggested Mum.

_____

48 Daniel asked, "Where are we going tomorrow?"

_____

49 "Do I have to go to school today?" questioned Jay.

_____

50 Dad had an idea, "Let's go for a bike ride."

_____

4

List five **prepositions**.

51–55 _____ _____ _____

_____ _____

Complete the table with **comparative** and **superlative adjectives**.

56–60

Adjectives	Comparative adjectives	Superlative adjectives
heavy		heaviest
good		
stupid		

Write a **definition** for each of these words.

61 eminent _____

62 imminent _____

63 ensure _____

64 insure _____

65 bought _____

66 brought _____

From which country do you think these words were borrowed?

67 deluxe _____

68 macaroni _____

69 racquet _____

70 spaghetti _____

71 dachshund _____

Write four **onomatopoeic** words describing 'water'.

72–75 _____ _____

_____ _____

4

Write five **synonyms** for the word 'strange',

76–80 _____ _____ _____

_____ _____

5

Rewrite these sentences with their missing punctuation.

81–84 I can't do this anymore screamed Leah as she buried her head in her numeracy homework

_____

_____

4

85–91 Tyler asked What time is the clown arriving Quarter to four replied his mum

_____

_____

7

92–95 Towan Beach a private beach with perfect sand is set behind the Trewince Manor Hotel just a mile from Portscatho

_____

_____

4

Add a **phrase** to complete each sentence.

96 The gang, _____, stopped and listened.

97 The elephant sauntered _____ to the water hole.

98 Venus _____ sold many of her paintings online.

99 The small bedroom was _____.

100 The old man walked slowly _____.

5

Mixed paper 4

Wild Swans

The book, Wild Swans, *details the life of Jung Chang, her mother and her grandmother growing up in China. In this extract, Jung Chang tells us about her early school experiences.*

In the autumn of 1958, when I was six, I started going to a primary school about 20 minutes' walk from home, mostly along muddy cobbled back alleys. Every day on my way to and from school, I screwed up my eyes to search every inch of ground for broken nails, rusty cogs, and any other metal objects that had been trodden into mud between the cobbles. These were for feeding into furnaces to produce steel, which was my major occupation. Yes, at the age of six, I was involved in steel production, and had to compete with my schoolmates at handing in the most scrap iron. All around me uplifting music blared from loudspeakers, and there were banners, posters, and huge slogans painted on the walls proclaiming 'Long Live the Great Leap Forward!' and 'Everybody, Make Steel!' Although I did not fully understand why, I knew that Chairman Mao had ordered the nation to make a lot of steel. In my school, crucible-like vats had replaced some of our cooking woks and were sitting on the giant stoves in the kitchen. All our scrap iron was fed into them, including the old woks, which had now been broken to bits. The stoves were kept permanently lit – until they melted down. Our teachers took turns feeding firewood into them around the clock, and stirring the scraps in the vats with a huge spoon. We did not have many lessons, as the teachers were too preoccupied with the vats. So were the older, teenage children. The rest of us were organised to clean the teachers' apartments and babysit for them.

I remember visiting a hospital once with some other children to see one of our teachers who had been seriously burned when molten iron had splashed onto her arms. Doctors and nurses in white coats were rushing around frantically. There was a furnace on the hospital grounds, and they had to feed logs into it all the time, even when they were performing operations, and right through the night.

Shortly before I started going to school, my family had moved from the old vicarage into a special compound, which was the centre of government for the province. A huge furnace was erected in the parking lot. At night the sky was lit up, and the noise of the crowds around the furnace could be heard 300 yards away in my room. My family's woks went into the furnace, together with all our cast-iron cooking utensils. We did not suffer from their loss, as we did not need them anymore. No private cooking was allowed now, and everybody had to eat in the canteen. The furnaces were insatiable. Gone was my parents' bed, a soft, comfortable one with iron springs. Gone also were the iron railings from the city pavements, and anything else that was iron. I hardly saw my parents for months. They often did not come home at all, as they had to make sure the temperature in their office furnaces never dropped.

It was at this time that Mao gave full vent to his half-baked dream … and ordered steel output to be doubled in one year – from 5.35 million tons in 1957 to 10.7 million in 1958. But instead of trying to expand the proper steel industry with skilled workers, he decided to get the whole population to take part … It was officially estimated that nearly 100 million peasants were pulled out of agricultural work and into steel production. They had been the labour force producing much of the country's food.

From *Wild Swans* by Jung Chang

Answer these questions.

1 How old was Jung Chang when she began primary school?

_____

2 What is meant by a 'major occupation' on line 7?

_____

3–5 In your own words, describe Jung Chang's walk to school.

_____

_____

_____

_____

6–8 How did school for Jung Chang differ from the school life you have?
Give three examples.

_____

_____

_____

_____

9–10 What do the words **a** 'preoccupied' (line 19) and **b** 'frantically' (line 26)
mean in the context of this extract?

a 'preoccupied' means _____

b 'frantically' means _____

11 What evidence in the extract is there that the furnaces were
dangerous?

_____

12–13 What is shocking about the information in paragraph two (lines 23 to
28). Why?

_____

_____

14 Where did Jung Chang move to before starting school?

_____

15 Why weren't the Chang family concerned when their cooking things were put in the furnaces?

_____

16 Why did Jung Chang's parents sometimes not come home at night?

_____

17–18 What do you think the effect was of moving the labour force from the land to steel production?

_____

_____

19–20 Do you think that China was a happy place to live during this time? Why?

_____

_____

_____

(20)

Add _ery_, _ory_ or _ary_ to complete these words.

21 extraordin_____

22 contradict_____

23 batt_____

24 satisfact_____

25 deliv_____

(5)

Write a **homophone** for each of these words.

26 bread _____

27 choose _____

28 horse _____

29 moose _____

30 rung _____

(5)

Add the missing vowels to complete the words.

31 b __ n j __   32 b __ f f __ l __ o

33 c __ c __ __   34 v __ t __ m __ n

35 d r __ m __

Change these words into their **singular** form.

36 hooves   _____   37 wolves   _____

38 fishwives _____   39 penknives _____

40 wharves   _____

5

Write each of these **adverbs** in a sentence.

41 stupidly

_____

42 overtime

_____

43 latterly

_____

44 eastwards

_____

45 deliberately

_____

5

Write two words for each of the following word classes.

46–47 abstract noun   _____   _____

48–49 pronoun   _____   _____

50–51 connective   _____   _____

52–53 superlative adjective   _____   _____

54–55 verb   _____   _____

10

Write an **adjectival phrase** for each of these **nouns.**

56 saucepan   _____

57 gate   _____

58 coconut   _____

59 animal   _____

60 mobile phone   _____   5

What is the **root word** in each of these words?

61 foreigner   _____   62 independent   _____

63 incidentally   _____   64 acquaintance   _____

65 undoubtedly   _____   5

Write the meaning of each of these **metaphorical** expressions.

66 to be hard of hearing

_____

67 to hold one's tongue

_____

68 to rain cats and dogs

_____

69 to be heavy eyed

_____

70 to be the apple of one's eye

_____   5

Write these **abbreviations** in full.

71 abbr.   _____   72 BC   _____

73 adj.   _____   74 vol.   _____

75 no.   _____   5

Write two or three **antonyms** for each word.

76–77 kind

_____   _____

2

78–80 smooth

_____   _____   _____

3

Rewrite this passage correctly.

81–100

It was a hot morning Mum opened Jacobs curtains before turning to him Today is a special day Get up quickly and she left

Five minutes later he was having his breakfast I am impressed stated Mum I wish you were this quick every day

Where are we off to asked Jacob

Nowhere ... but weve a visitor she smiled

_____

_____

_____

_____

_____

_____

_____

_____

20

_____